KENDAL

PAST & PRESENT

BRITAIN

Kendal

Past & Present

John Marsh

SUTTON PUBLISHING

Sutton Publishing Limited
Phoenix Mill · Thrupp · Stroud
Gloucestershire · GL5 2BU

First published 2003

Copyright © John Marsh, 2003

British Library Cataloguing in Publication Data
A catalogue record for this book is available from the
British Library.

ISBN 0-7509-3397-6

Typeset in 10.5/13.5 Photina.
Typesetting and origination by
Sutton Publishing Limited.
Printed and bound in England by
J.H. Haynes & Co. Ltd, Sparkford.

Half-title page photograph: Westmorland Step & Garland Group at the Medieval Millennium Market, Kendal, 2001.

Title page photograph: Abbot Hall park entrance in the early twentieth century with gates to match the iron railings which have surrounded the park since its acquisition by the Borough Council in 1897. (The Castle, framed by the arch, was acquired at the same time with monies given on the winding up of the Savings Bank.) The use of the park 'out of hours' was forbidden in by-laws which were enforced by the Kendal Borough Police.

CONTENTS

The top of Finkle Street in the centre of the town. This is where Highgate and Stricklandgate meet. The Pump Inn, with Crock Lane on the left with the lamp and Finkle Street as a narrow lane on the right, ha the Fish Market at its rear. The fish stones and the town well can both be seen. All of this has been cleare away to make a wider entrance to Finkle Street which was fitted with a modern shelter in recent decade (see also page 92). It is hard to imagine that the narrow Finkle Street seen here was the main road t Scotland which carried armies and coach traffic. It's rather different to today's M6.

INTRODUCTION

For nearly two decades I have had the pleasure of taking groups of people in and out of the nooks and crannies of medieval Kendal in what have been termed 'Historic Town Walks'. The interest shown in the history of this royal borough has never ceased to amaze me. The parties I have shown round have been from America and Germany, France and, of course, the United Kingdom. Many groups have been 'local' from the WIs and other groups, of which there are many in the area. Frequently I have been asked for a book to accompany the walk. 'Why don't you write a history of Kendal?' has been a frequent question.

This book is not a history of Kendal, although a lot of the history is included. To write a history of Kendal would require the services of an academic historian and archaeologists, and I am neither. As a town guide I discovered that the true story of Kendal has been wrongly written for well over a century and much of it has just been made up. In the early days of the town walks I thought that local people would be upset to find that their long-held knowledge of the town was based on fairy stories. But as more and more of the true story of the town came to light the walkers appreciated having their knowledge updated. A copy of the market charter which tells of problems with the market during the plague years in the sixteenth century, came to light in Levens Hall in 1989, the year of celebrations of 800 years of Kendal Market. Such finds are rare, and until more is discovered no one can attempt a true history of the town. There have been archaeological investigations but, unfortunately, these, at the time of going to press, have mostly remained unpublished. Again without archaeological detail a history of the town cannot be written.

I think that Kendalians are now happy in the knowledge that Queen Katherine Parr was not born in Kendal Castle, as had been put about in Victorian times. Dr David Starkey, the Tudor historian, who was born and brought up in Kendal, has confirmed this. The Kendal Civic Society invited Dr Starkey to give a talk in Kendal recently and he answered many questions from his capacity audience. Explaining the detail of this to a party on the Castle hill has extended many a Castle Kendal walk. And yet many old Kendalians resent the 'rewriting of history' that is being undertaken at present. The town's story was so riddled with myth and fable that the job of town guide was difficult from the start. American audiences were not happy with 'maybe' and 'possibly' in connection with so many sites in the town.

When my turn came to retire from the position of town guide my place was taken by Trevor Hughes, who is quickly making a name for himself as an authority on the town. Trevor's uncle was a renowned authority on the history not only of Kendal but also of Cumbria and was the County Historic Buildings Officer until his retirement. Trevor has since inherited the large collection of photographs put together by his uncle. He has kindly let me have copies of many of these pictures of old Kendal, and some are included in the pages of this book. He has also put together a CD-ROM of his uncle's collection which he is selling on behalf of the Kendal Deaf Centre Extension Fund. Both Trevor and I have reason to be thankful for the existence of the Deaf Centre as we both have deaf offspring that have gained much by being involved in such a place. My son, who was born deaf, is now chairman of the Sports Centre Committee. Any profits from this book are being given to the Deaf Centre Extension Fund.

And so historic town walks, old photographs of Kendal and the Kendal Deaf Centre make up the *raison d'être* of this book. I hope it will be a worthy companion to the dozen or so old photograph books I have compiled for Sutton Publishing since 1991. I must also thank my readers who pressure me to do more (and suggest titles for me to write about). I am sorry this is not the history of Kendal so much in demand. I am not the man for that and I suggest pressure for such a much-needed book is put elsewhere.

John Marsh
July 2003

1

South Kendal & Kirkland

This aerial view of Kirkland dates from the First World War, as the parish hall can clearly be seen. The Holy Well of St Mary can be seen top left; this became the Anchorite Well after the Reformation. The seventeenth-century historian Machell tells us that a church older than the parish church was situated near this well. Kirkbarrow House (recently demolished) can be seen and Kirkbarrow itself was the site of allotment gardens. This is the most ancient part of Kendal. The Domesday Book names it as Kirkbie in Strickland. A village by a holy well may have existed in pre-Christian times, but only archaeologists can help the town on this. The Normans arrived in Kendal in about 1080 and, as elsewhere, set about replacing the old order with their own. A new church, the present parish church, was built and a motte and bailey castle built overlooking ancient Kirkby, which was renamed Kirkby Kendal (the church town in the Kent valley). The ancient Kirkland remained separate from the Borough of Kendal until 1908.

Natland is gradually being absorbed into the town of Kendal, and is now largely a suburb of the town. The church has changed its appearance on a number of occasions, having been rebuilt for various reasons. The church in the old photograph (left) was built in 1825 but proved 'cold on Sundays and . . . so damp' that villagers stopped attending and a new church by Paley and Austin of Lancaster was built in 1910. The Paley and Austin church can be seen below. It has proved to be the centre of village life with a vibrant congregation.

Above and opposite: Nether Bridge toll house. The junction of the Natland and Burton roads was the site of a toll bar for the Heronsyke to Eamont Bridge Turnpike Trust (see *c.* 1870 view, opposite above). Its new road, now the Burton road, met the medieval (or earlier) road to the south (now the Natland road). Local road users avoided the toll bars in any way possible, so the turnpike trusts started to fail. They were taken over by the quarter sessions and later the county council (in 1889). Assets such as toll bar houses were sold off by the new county council. The Nether Bridge toll house came into private hands, was demolished and replaced with a house of similar appearance, as can be seen in the early twentieth-century view (left) and the recent picture, which also shows the traffic island which is Kendal's answer to a modern problem – traffic pollution.

The Old Grammar School in Church Walk, Kirkland was founded in 1525 as a church school run by the monks of St Mary's Abbey at York. When the abbey was closed during the Dissolution of the Monasteries in 1539 not only the parish church but also the school went into decline through lack of patronage. The latter ceased to exist for nearly fifty years until the Philipson family of Crook, benefactors with Church lands, refounded the school in the Elizabethan grammar school style in 1588. Above is a late nineteenth-century view of the school building after its transformation into three houses once the Old Grammar School had left for a new site on the Lound. The modern picture shows how little things have changed during the twentieth century, although half of the building has become part of the Museum of Lakeland Life and Industry.

The new grammar school on the Lound has been much enlarged since it was founded here in 1889 when the Blue Coat School charity merged with the grammar school charity to construct this building on land given by the Wakefield family. Above is the original school building, which was much enlarged as education became a government responsibility. The buildings below now house a comprehensive school which has adopted the old name of Kirkby Kendal.

The Howard Home for Orphans no longer exists. Now the buildings are the Stonecross Manor Hotel. The orphanage was founded in 1865 by the Hon. Mrs Howard of Levens Hall and originally housed forty girls who were trained for domestic service and other employment. Over the years the buildings have been an old folks' home and, more recently, housed Yugoslavian refugees escaping their terrible civil war. When the original orphanage was being built a Bronze Age burial site was uncovered, which attests to the continued occupation of the Kent valley since 2,000 years before the Romans. The name Stonecross refers to the site of a medieval stone wayside cross which stood nearby, but it has not survived. The site is now marked with a small boulder with a cross scratched into it.

The vicarage for Kendal parish church was originally next to the church, but a new vicarage was built just off the Milnthorpe road in the middle of the nineteenth century and the curates were housed in the old vicarage. The new vicarage, seen above, was a fine building. However, by the 1970s it had become the property of the Cumbria County Council Education Department, which, announcing that the building was unsafe, pulled it down in 1974. The site became a wilderness, as can be seen below. Today it is difficult to understand why such an asset was destroyed instead of being redeveloped, but this state of affairs marks the first of many demolitions approved by South Lakeland District planners from 1974 when the council was formed.

The Romney House in Milnthorpe Road was named after local man George Romney, who became an internationally important artist. He was born at Cocken near Dalton-in-Furness in 1734 and became apprenticed to Christopher Steel in 1755 as a portrait painter, where, with Daniel Gardner, he became part of the Kendal School of portrait painters in a cottage in a yard off Stricklandgate (see page 111). Romney left the north as his fame increased and did not return until 1799 when his health was failing. He was nursed by his wife in this house until 1802 when he died. *Opposite*: Romney House, 2003.

The main street from near the church gates looking south. Kirkland was the name of the main street as well as the township. All the cottages and shops on the left side were pulled down in August 1904 leaving the parish church school exposed to the main street. The clearance carried on from the church to the Nether Bridge on one side only, leaving the west side to be redeveloped in sections, the main development being the building of Crabtree's Garage at the end of the First World War.

Kirkland looking towards Highgate from the Chapel Lane/Peppercorn Lane crossing as seen in the 1880s and today, showing an ancient street used by modern traffic on a quiet day. Chapel Lane became Capper Lane after the Reformation, but there were not enough hat makers to support the change, so it reverted to its old name. The lane, according to old maps and Machell's reporting of the situation in the seventeenth century, led to the chapel by the holy well. Beyond Chapel Lane was a ford over the Blind Beck, the boundary with Market Kendal or the Baron's Kendal (neither name was ever used), which became Soutergate in medieval times, and later Highgate.

The Anchorite Well, the site of the centre of ancient Kendal. This is a well that never runs dry and would have been a place of importance from the beginning of the occupation of the valley. It acquired cult status and was probably a holy place in the centuries before Christianity. The Romans would have known of it, and among other gods the Earth Mother goddess would have been worshipped here. In the early years of Christianity the cult of the Earth Mother was transmuted into that of the Mother of God, St Mary, hence St Mary's Well. There are many mentions of St Mary's Well and its syke (stream) in medieval documents, and when a new church was built by the river in the thirteenth century great trouble was taken to route the syke through the new church site – where it runs today. At the Reformation much effort went into the destruction of places such as this with connections to earlier religions, and many names of places were changed. St Mary's Well syke became the Brockbeck and St Mary's Lane became Kirkbarrow Lane. The site in more recent times has been surrounded by a large housing estate, become the site of a fish and chip shop, and was provided with a bus stop and at one time a gents' urinal. The late nineteenth-century view above shows the rural nature of the place at that time and the picture opposite shows the scene today. The well is still there, in spite of everything.

Cross Lane is now a spur off Chapel Lane, which from early days was a road from Kirkland to St Mary's Well. In 1692 Machell recorded that there was a church older than the parish church at the head of Chapel Lane. Above can be seen the building that stood at the junction of Chapel Lane and Cross Lane. Its history was never investigated, and it was part of the postwar slum clearance scheme under which much of old Kendal was swept away. Its replacement is shown left.

Chapel Lane in the nineteenth century was a narrow, winding lane which had acquired the name Capper. As it supported more pubs than hat makers the new name did not last; the old name was brought back into use and a small non-conformist chapel built.
Left: Chapel Lane, 2003.

The maltkiln cottages, which were situated between the Nether Bridge and the entrance to the Nether Bridge ford, were obviously industrial buildings given a new lease of life as houses. They were demolished in 1906 along with much of the housing on the river side of Kirkland. The scene today shows northbound traffic against a neat background of wall and shrubs. The wall leading on to the bridge is probably the only feature common to each picture.

The vicarage lodge was at the entrance of the drive to the first Kendal vicarage next to the church. It is reputed to have been built by the Websters of Kendal. When its days as a lodge came to an end it became a small shop. Then it was demolished to make way for a mound for floral displays – the Queen's Golden Jubilee display is shown below.

The Abbot Hall (right) in the early years of the twentieth century when the borough council did not have any idea what to do with it and were seriously considering demolition. The building was once the town house of the Wilsons of Dallam. It was built by Colonel George Wilson after he demolished the medieval Abbot Hall used by the Abbot of St Mary's Abbey, York. The borough council was given Abbot Hall and its park (along with Kendal Castle and its hill) after the winding up of the Savings Bank, with left-over funds being used to benefit the town. From 1896 until the Second World War the shoe-string economics of the borough council had nothing to spare to preserve either the castle or the Abbot Hall and both suffered as a result. Just after the war a fund was set up with the borough treasurer, Alfred Wainwright, as treasurer, but it took the generosity of a private person to endow the restoration of the Abbot Hall as an art gallery.

Mr P. Scott of the Provincial Insurance Co. provided many millions to Kendal over the years of the company's existence. The picture below shows how little the scene has apparently changed in a hundred years, although the building has been almost completely rebuilt in that time.

The Cropper Memorial in the corner of Abbot Hall Park is to James Cropper, the last Member of Parliament for Kendal and the first chairman of Westmorland County Council. The slate memorial is as modest as can be and carries the motto 'Love all men and fear no man' on its face and 'Love, Joy, Zeal, Hope and Faith' on a tree of life on the reverse. James Cropper's birth and death dates have served to test school children since the erection of the stone, as they are in Roman numerals – MDCCCXXIII (1823) and MDCCCC (1900). The family lives on in Burneside where they run the vast paper mills there.

2

The Canal & River Kent

The canal and the River Kent wend their ways through both the church lands and the market town of Kendal. The river gives its name to the town. The picture shows the terminus of the Lancaster to Kendal Canal in the late nineteenth century. The top basin at Canal Head can clearly be seen and the arches that permitted barges to enter the canal warehouse (which are now built into the workshop of Gilkes & Gordon's engineering works) stand out on the canal basin side. Opened in 1819, the canal suffered a long decline following the arrival of the railway in the 1840s. All around Canal Head can be seen the industries which made Kendal prosperous following the canal's arrival. This is now a much changed scene. It would appear likely that the canal, which was closed in the 1940s and filled in during the 1950s, is to be reopened with a Canal Head basin on the castle side. A trip from Kendal to London by barge at 3 miles per hour would then be possible.

Change Bridge on the Lound with a crowded barge on a Whitsuntide trip (probably to Levens Park). The working barges were cleaned for this purpose as and when required. The crowds gather on the Change Bridge and the canal side to watch the event. The same scene today shows a filled-in canal and a restored Change Bridge which was a Kendal Civic Society project, as a first stage to the reopening of the Lancaster to Kendal Canal.

The Change Bridge in recent years. *Right*: the stonework of the bridge almost ready to fall down with trees growing through the masonry. *Below*: the same spot on 13 May 2002 with Dr John Satchell, chairman of the Civic Society, and Roger Bingham, chairman of South Lakeland District Council, declaring the restored bridge open to traffic (they used a horse to make the point). The bridge is unique in the county of Cumbria and was designed by the canal's architect, John Rennie, to allow the towing horse to change sides on the canal without being unfastened from the barge. A Kendal Civic Society plaque can be seen on the house wall behind where historian Trevor Hughes is recording the scene for posterity. The arrival of the restored waterway in the next few years will complete the scene, although horse-drawn barges are not expected on the revived canal.

The terminus of the canal at canal level (see also page 31), shows a barge loaded with what looks like manure, which is being unloaded into the adjoining market gardens. This scene is no more, but the large limestone coping stones at the canal edge can still be found.

Also at Canal Head is the house built for the canal manager, who is seen in the picture above with his wife and children in the garden, *c*. 1900. A hundred years later the house has changed somewhat, after being a school caretaker's house and a school store.

The canal ticket office on Canal Head north, in the nineteenth century (above) and today (below). The management of Messrs Gilkes and Gordon were aware of the importance of this little building when rebuilding their works and carefully included the ticket office in the new arrangements. If only others in Kendal had been so conservation minded!

endal Grammar School on the Lound (see pages 14 and 15). Sitting on the side of the River Kent, it verlooked the Lound Dam that provided water for the water wheels of the Low Mills through a leet, which an down the side of the Natland road. Above is an early twentieth-century view of the school which shows he Lound Dam blocking the course of the river, and below is the scene today following the removal of the am in the 1970s clearances to avoid flooding.

The riverside works of K Shoes on the Netherfield can be seen reflected in the water held back by the Loun
Dam. The water behind the dam, between Nether Bridge and the dam, became a favourite place for boating
Boating would be impossible today as the 1970s river works cleared the river bottom down to the limeston
sills over which it flows today. The K Shoes factory, now a factory shop, can just be seen through the trees.

The Nether Bridge ford is also a thing of the past. At the turn of the twentieth century (above) it was still being used to allow herds of animals and large loads on horse wagons to cross the river. Below is the scene today, photographed from the same place on Aynam Road.

Kendal parish church from the river, *c.* 1900. The wall on the left surrounds the pre-1860 vicarage which had become a home for the curates by that time. One wing of this interesting building, which was on the site of the medieval priests' house and which was swept away in the early decades of the twentieth century to make way for a parish hall, can just be seen. The church itself was completely restored in 1850 following centuries of underfunding and neglect after the Reformation. The riverside in those days led directly to the water level, almost a beach, which allowed children to play in the river in a manner not possible today.

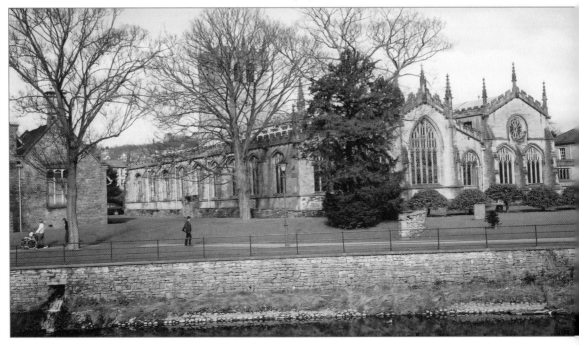

The Romney road footbridge, built in 1906–7, even saw use by small motor cars before it was replaced by a modern structure that now takes much of the traffic wishing to avoid Kendal town centre. A replica of the glorious Edwardian footbridge was erected at the top end of the town at the same time that the new road bridge was being erected.

Above: The Jennings Yard footbridge was replaced with a modern structure, following the loss of the original in a flood in 1898 when it was washed away to end up on the river bank by Wilkinson's piano works. The railings that kept people out of Abbot Hall Park can be seen but riverside railings (left) to keep people out of the river had yet to arrive. The river before and after the flood avoidance work is of interest. The channel was both widened and deepened, with the result that the River Kent has not flooded the town since the 1970s.

Above: Sledall Almshouses on Aynam Road were erected in 1887 to celebrate Queen Victoria's Golden Jubilee. Originally the residents had their own chapel on the end of the row, but in recent years this has been converted into more accommodation. John Sledall, who had fallen out with the vicar at New Hutton, built his charity almshouses in Kendal instead. Little has apparently changed here today.

Many reasons have been given as to why the steps to the river near the end of the Highgate yards were built. The reason most used is that they were wool washers' steps used by the wool trade in the various Highgate yards. In fact they were steps allowing access to water in the river for wool washing, washing clothes, drinking and bathing, as for most of their lives the buildings in the Highgate yards did not have a water supply (unless they had a well). When one considers that a town main sewer was emptied into the river just upriver of the steps, what exactly did the people collect in their buckets? The Highgate yards were cleared in a frenzy of postwar renewal and replaced with award-winning flats, which can be seen below. They were designed by Frederick Gibberd, who is more famous for the Catholic cathedral in Liverpool.

The Riverside, seen right in about 1905, includes the mixture of old buildings to be found at the end of Highgate yards. A set of steps to the river can be clearly seen. Halfway along was the common lodging house where visitors wiped their feet on leaving and, it was said, rat soup was on the menu. The river today is wider and in a deeper channel. In spite of Gibberd's flats, this is now a popular promenade avoiding the town traffic fumes.

St George's Church stands on a piece of land raised by nearly 6ft to escape the floods on the nearby river. The building by architects Websters of Kendal in the church commissioners' style of Early English Lancet has been altered a number of times. The twin towers were unsafe and were lowered to end up as mere stumps, and the east end gained a new chancel in 1907–11 when Paley and Austin of Lancaster were the architects (see also page 104–5). The lower picture shows a much changed scene.

3

Highgate

Highgate was called Soutergate in medieval times, which was generally understood to mean
'the main road to the south', until academics pointed out that it meant 'the road of the
shoemakers'. As both Ulverston and Kirkby-in-Furness have roads called Soutergate which
were the ancient roads to the south, does this mean that shoemakers in south Cumbria all
worked on the main road to the south?
Kendal Town Hall in its original form is seen here at the time that the borough council moved
from the Moot Hall in the market place to the Whitehall, erected on the corner of Lowther
Street and Highgate by the Websters. Built as a building for public meetings and called the
White Hall, it originally had a cupola which was replaced with a clock tower in 1861 after
the corporation had purchased the building in 1858/9. In the 1890s the building was too
small and was extended on the land occupied by the wine shop. Alderman Bindloss of Castle
Green made a huge bequest in order that the work could be carried out.

The Dowker Hospital seen above in about 1900, was a charity founded in 1831 to provide accommodation for six good and chaste Kendal females over fifty years of age. The rather delightful hospital building at the entrance to Abbot Hall park was designed by the Websters of Kendal in 1825 and lasted until the borough council Highgate clearances in the 1970s when it was removed to make a road which carries the Dowker name. The front portico of the building can now be found at the top of the new Webster Yard development in Highgate.

The Royal Oak Inn (above, left), with the gas light over the entrance to Yard 123, was a fine seventeenth-century structure which, as can be seen below, still exists but has been much altered. Page 51 shows how 'improvements' have changed things at the back where Yard 123 Highgate no longer exists. The view south from Highgate Bank to the boundary with Kirkland can still be recognised, in spite of the traffic.

Left: Yard 24 Highgate, or Wilson's Yard, was the access to the rear of Titus Wilson's premises, but it no longer exists, having been absorbed into the new shop that replaced that famous Kendal building.

Below: It proved impossible to take the view from the same site as above, as much of the yard is now inside the new building as shop space. The doorway into the shop replaced the yard entrance.

Yard 123 Highgate had the Royal Oak Inn at its head and allowed access on to Highgate through the south end of that ancient inn, the name of which celebrates King Charles II's escape from the Parliamentary Army when he hid in an oak tree. (One would have thought that as the Restoration of the Monarchy brought so many benefits to the Royal Borough that this inn would have survived the pressures of commercial enterprise.) The yard was swept away in the postwar slum clearances and replaced with a modern development which was truncated by Dowker Lane and the award-winning Riverside flats.

Captain French's Lane is an ancient road out of Highgate which had the name The Ratten Row. The story goes that when Captain French took a house at the Highgate end of the road the inhabitants decided that Captain French's Lane would be a more appropriate name to celebrate the Civil War captain. In modern times the traffic problems of the town have been turned into the chance for humour in the form of a no parking sign in the lane.

Groves Yard 97 Highgate was described by John Curwen as 'having always been considered one of the nicest in Kendal – also Miss Isabella Lickbarrow the poetess resided there'. That was in 1900 when Mr Curwen could not have had any idea what the post-1947 planners would inflict on the scene. As can be seen, like Yard 123 earlier, it can hardly be described as an improvement. It is no wonder that Dr Starkey, of TV fame, on a visit to his home town in 2002 was quite scathing on the efforts of the planners, saying, 'it could have been like York'.

Yard 126 Highgate was called 'Two Seater Yard' after the mason William Holme who lived in the yard and erected two stone seats either side of the entrance for the use of passers by. Holme was an early partner of architect Francis Webster when he arrived in Kendal in 1788.

The view below shows how the old yard has been done away with to make room for a car park and adjoining modern offices.

Highgate meets All Hallows Lane in 1914, before the lane was widened. A Kendal Borough policeman stands at the roadside observing the goings on in a time-honoured manner. Today's modern clutter – the CCTV camera on the corner, the smashed window boarded up and the 'drinking prohibited' notice are an enormous contrast. The Thompson family, who ran the china shop in Dolphin House, is the same family that joined Websters the architects to form Thompson and Webster in the early nineteenth century.

Highgate in the 1880s shows a busy scene before the days of the internal combustion engine. Youngsters could, and did, wander in the street in safety and out-of-town locals did their shopping from their trap parked outside the shop. On the left is Webster's 'Bank of Westmorland' which was built in answer to the Quaker banks that had started in the town in the early nineteenth century. Built in 1834, it is still recognisable today. Only the traffic, Kendal's major problem, changes the scene dramatically, although many other details have changed as a close examination will reveal.

All Hallows Lane from the top looking towards
the town hall, before the road widening of
1914, and today. The lane in medieval times
was called Holy Hill and led to the now lost
Church of the Holy Cross and All Hallows,
which was in the corner where Beast Banks can
be found today. It is rather amazing, in view of
what has happened in other parts of the town,
that the name has survived. The church
building survived until the seventeenth century.

Kendal Town Hall and Highgate in the late nineteenth century, in a continuation of the view seen on page 57. The streets belonged to the people and motor vehicle pollution had yet to arrive. The modern scene is partly obscured by 'white van man' – a circumstance too common in our age. It is unfortunate that many people consider that a main street full of polluting motor vehicles is a sign of prosperity when the opposite is the truth; many townspeople go to great expense to shop elsewhere.

The extension of Kendal Town Hall in the 1890s required the demolition of the wine and spirits merchant's next door which had been the Wheatsheaf Inn before that. Mrs Bindloss, widow of the councillor who contributed most of the cost of the improvements, is seen here laying the foundation stone of the new extension, which was completed in time for Queen Victoria's Diamond Jubilee.

The Fleece Inn Yard and the Old Shambles get constantly confused, even by the businesses situated there. Here we see a building that spanned both – Richardson's Westmorland Churn Works, which became Stainton's Garage and house, is seen above in its churn works days and below as the house occupied for many years by the Stainton family. Its address should be Old Shambles.

The Old Shambles is where the slaughtering
of animals and the butchers' shops were
moved to in 1779 when Alderman Petty
built forty shops to provide the town with a
more convenient location for the goings on
then associated with the butcher's trade.
Above we see the scene in the late nineteenth
century when the butchers had gone and the
dye works of Messrs Whitaker and Co., which
had started life as the 1779 Butcher's Arms,
dominated the scene with a backdrop of the
Fellside. Today it is a totally different scene,
dominated by a car park and council flats.
After the postwar slum clearances Frederick
Gibberd's award-winning buildings shared
the glory of the Waterside Flats. The butchers
took their work into a new Shambles
between Market Place and Finkle Street, but
the mess they made there caused the
borough council to open an abbatoir at the
Canal Head in about 1850.

Cock Lane is not a name used today, but
neither is Fleece Yard, shown on the right in
the late nineteenth century. It was on the
opposite side of the Fleece Inn to the Old
Shambles. Up until the mid-nineteenth century
this was Cock Lane, named after Alderman
William Cock, mercer, who lived in a house
that became a seedman's business for Messrs
Webb (see page 64). However, in mid-Victorian
Kendal it was decided that the name Fleece
Yard would be more appropriate for this
narrow alley in which generations of night
duty policemen had slept away the night hours
in the boiler room of the Fleece Inn, the door of
which was left open to welcome the tired
keepers of the peace, an old hotel chair
provided.

Opposite and above: The Fleece Inn was originally in the Old Shambles, but it was extended on to Highgate when the house on the front street became vacant. The name Golden Fleece was on the original sign, but this became the Fleece with the passing of time. It is famous for nothing in particular, other than its architectural style as a timber-framed lathe and plaster building typical of many in the town at one time. The old building (opposite) looks as it did until recent modernisation altered its appearance. Next door are the premises of Webb's (established in 1910), where Webb's Wonderful Lettuce was the worldwide famous product, the seeds for which could be bought over the counter. Originally this building belonged to Alderman Cock, who gave his name to Cock Lane, the alley between Webb's shop and the Fleece (see page 63). The improvements which have been allowed in recent years can be seen above.

The Sandes Hospital Almshouses and the Bluecoats School, *c.* 1900. In the late seventeenth century Thomas Sandes founded a hospital for poor widows in a building at the front of a burgage croft he had acquired in Highgate. However, the building that is seen nowadays is not all it seems, as much of the plot was rebuilt by a Miles Thompson, architect and councillor, in 1852. The row of almshouses seen above date from that time. The school at the top of the yard is probably earlier but was much improved in 1849 when a weaving floor was removed and lancet windows installed. Today on the left are the backs of the flats and houses that now make up one side of Websters Yard, the most modern of Kendal's yards, built on land once used by Francis Webster as a builder's yard.

The Westmorland Garage in Highgate run by Messrs Atkinson and Griffin, 1910. Monkhouse & Son, glass and china dealers, can be seen at no. 60 and the Bank of Westmorland is set back next door. Today the scene is much changed.

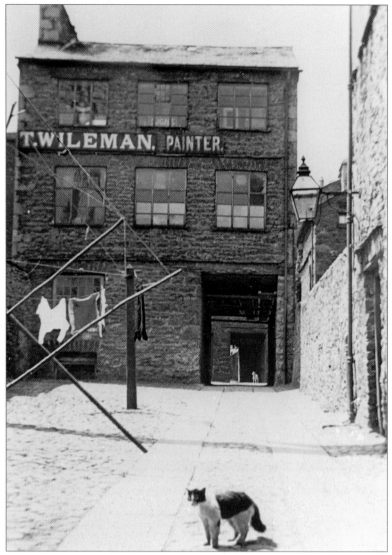

New Bank Yard took its name from a bank set up by a group of Quaker businessmen at the Highgate top of the yard. Entrance to the yard was by a narrow alleyway – so narrow many Kendalians did not know it existed. The nineteenth-century development of the town centre yard was made by building over the original yard, the arches thus formed making a highly interesting place. The borough council and later the South Lakeland District Council had other ideas for the piece of ground adjoining their newly planned offices. They would build a multi-storey car park on the site of New Bank Yard. A relative of the founder of the New Bank raised his voice in complaint: although he did not succeed in his fight against municipality, he did succeed in forming the Kendal Civic Society with a group of like-minded people. They gathered together to stop the mindless demolition which was being carried out in Kendal in the name of planning and commercial enterprise. The civic society now has national standing and even has members sitting on committees organised by the local planning authority. The loss of the New Bank Yard has been more than rewarded by the foundation of the Kendal Civic Society. The picture shows one of the lost courts – Wileman's Court (and cat) – with other courts to be seen through the arch.

4

On the Fellside

The time gun, Serpentine Woods, in the nineteenth century. Kendal is situated in a valley with, on the west, a limestone fell which allowed the early town to develop, as there was an ample supply of water from the limestone. The earliest parts of Kendal, apart from the Roman fort in the valley bottom, are sited on the limestone. On the top of the limestone fell, where the Kendal Golf Club can now be found, are the Serpentine Woods, planted in the eighteenth century by the Kendal Fell Trust. It is in this wood that the trust sited an old canon on top of a gunpowder store building and this was fired each day at 1 p.m. Curwen records that the gun was lent by the War Office to the corporation; it was an 18-pounder, 9ft long, and weighed 42cwts. From 1873 it was fired by an electrical switch from a shop in town. The original time gun was taken to Abbot Hall Park and, sited on a suitable gun carriage, graced the park until the 1940s when it was taken for wartime scrap.

Kendal Golf Club is sited on land called from ancient times the Dob Freer – an ancient piece of wasteland that was a common to the people of Kendal. A golf club, founded in 1891 on Kendal Race Course, was joined with a club founded in 1897 which, in 1907, when the Kendal Fell Trust came to an end, took over the land next to the Serpentine Woods as a new course. The arguments have continued ever since, as walkers enjoying their common rights have to avoid golf balls hit by members of a golf club using the same land. Kendal Golf Club has prospered over the years. Above is the first (1893) clubhouse made of corrugated iron and opposite is the golf club premises today – the highest licensed premises in Kendal with a view so magnificent that, it is said, many matches were won by drawing visitors' attention to it.

Kendal's first hospital was a private one built by James Cropper in memory of Fanny Alison Cropper, his wife, in 1870. It is seen above in about 1900. The building remained in use as a hospital until 1991 when the present Westmorland General Hospital was opened. It became a part of Westmorland County Hospital on the other side of Captain French's Lane from the early twentieth century and it now houses a nursery school.

Greenside, *c.* 1900, and in recent times. It was here that Postman Pat was born along with all the other characters that make up the world-famous series of children's stories. Nearby Beast Banks post office is the post office the Postman Pat series is based on (see page 76). The parked cars below show a major problem not unique to Kendal, but they do clutter the town.

Left: Westmorland County Hospital in its first form, designed by the architect John Flavel Curwen, was opened in 1908. Over the years demand for its services grew and it expanded as a result. In the late 1980s further expansion became very difficult, so a new general hospital was built on the Burton road. There was much discussion as to what to do with the old building, but in the end, despite its architectural qualities, it was demolished. The picture opposite below shows the demolition of Curwen's hospital in 1994. Below is the private nursing home which is now on the site. The tower from the old hospital's staircase has been built into the new home.

Beast Bank post office will have ceased to exist by the time this book is published. Despite public outcry against closure, the privatised Royal Mail has decided that the post office which was the inspiration behind author John Cunliffe's famous books on Postman Pat, will be closed. This photograph shows Beast Bank post office in the week before its closure, with the last postmaster, Mike Malloy, standing beside the postbox. It will be sadly missed by the modern inhabitants of Greendale – sorry, Greenside – and another interesting part of Kendal will be no more. The Civic Society has promised that the premises will be provided with a plaque to commemorate the site of this world-famous post office.

Beast Banks for many years had a little shop on the corner with Belmont. Above is the shop when it was being run by the Dixon family. In recent years this was a bacon wholesaler and later a sweet shop, but today, see below, the shop has become part of the adjoining house.

Cliff Terrace was built in 1851, originally to be called Cliffside Terrace. The fine, large, limestone houses, with their own gardens in front with an extension on the lower side of the front lane, were a sign of the increasing prosperity of Kendal since the arrival of the canal. A mixture of houses provided a different terrace to many seen in other towns where uniformity of design was very popular. The view today has changed little in 150 years, except of course for the car parking.

The top of Entry Lane in the nineteenth century was very different to the modern view. The large block of flats and houses, which blended into the rest of the Fellside, has been swept away to be replaced with what were originally council flats. The railings at the top of the lane appear to be the same on both pictures, as are the wall and arched entrance on Low Fellside, but trees now hide the new flats. This is one of Kendal's most ancient of market place lanes, said by some to be the border of the huge market place from medieval days. It takes its name from the market cross which stood in Stricklandgate and included the call stain (or stone) from which all public announcements were made, its original name being Stanes Entry.

The junction of Queens Road and Serpentine Road. Queens Road was built on the line of the tramway built from the quarries on Helsfell to Windermere Road when the prison and the poorhouse were being built. In the 1880s Queens Road was extended from Windermere Road to Serpentine Terrace. The modern view gives the impression that Serpentine Woods have extended on to the Fellside.

All Hallows Lane has changed a lot since this picture was taken. This is the area of the medieval Church of the Holy Cross and All Hallows, which was closed at the Reformation. It was, it is thought, the market place church for the medieval market and All Hallows Lane, as Holy Hill formed a boundary. It is also part of the Nethergraveship of Kendal. People do not stand in groups in the road any more.

Beast Banks is a steep lane out of the market area. It takes its name from the cattle and sheep market and open slaughtering place, which probably dates from when a baron lived in the motte and bailey castle at its head. The killing of beasts gradually drifted down the hill into Highgate where new premises were built for butchers and slaughterers around the Newbiggin. The main road to Ulverston and Furness came this way, as did the coaches in their day. There is a small figure on the eaves above the first-floor window of the house on the right of both pictures. This is said to be Miles Thompson, the architect who built most of the row down the hill from the bow-fronted house. The figure above the bow windows was recently replaced by the Kendal Civic Society when the original blew off in high winds.

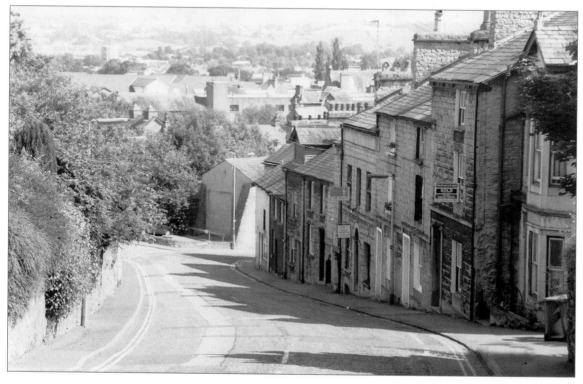

The house and lamp-post called 'Dawson's lighthouse' in Low Fellside has become the stuff of legend since an old picture was published in the *Westmorland Gazette* showing this house at the junction of Low Fellside and Middle Lane. Apparently Dawson lived in the house and was a regular visitor to the Black Swan public house at the foot of Beast Banks, from where there is a direct view of the lamp-post clearly shown on the old photograph. Dawson, the worse for drink, navigated his way home by the illuminated street lamp. Dawson's lamp became known as 'Dawson's lighthouse' and another of the Fellside stories was born. The new picture shows that the street lamp is no more and Dawson's house has gone.

On the Fellside among the poor-quality housing was a limestone well that had to be closed to prevent disease. The Public Health Acts and a piped water supply did much to improve the health of the area. However, the closure of the well left locals without a meeting place. A lot of romantic nonsense has been written about the Fellside, and the well is often featured. It was a dirty, infrequent water supply which gave typhoid to its many users. Many Kendalians could not find its site today, but possibly the picture below might help their search among Mr Gibberd's award-winning housing.

The Syke on Fellside was a much-photographed lane which ran down the hillside. This rarely seen nineteenth-century view is as good as any. The road had been roughly paved by this time, but it was a lane more suited to cats than children. The vacant chair on the left seems to indicate that an adult who had been taking the air decided she did not want to have her picture taken. There has been housing on Fellside since medieval times to house the people who worked in the market place, which has been much replaced over the centuries. By the twentieth century it had become a bad example of private social housing, a slum where the exploited rented poor accommodation. It was swept away after the Second World War as compulsory purchase orders were served on reluctant landlords. But was its replacement visually any better?

Helsfell Hall is the name given to three separate buildings, which has caused much confusion for over a hundred years. The remains of the first Helsfell Hall are evident in both photographs. This was the home of the Briggs family, who were cousins of the Philipsons of Crook, the local barons from medieval times. When the English Civil War in the seventeenth century divided the country the Philipsons were Royalists and the Briggs were Roundheads (or Parliamentarians). At the end of the Civil War the Briggs family lost everything as Captain Briggs had been more than a nuisance to his landlord cousin Robin, 'the devil' Philipson. The hall was stripped and a new Helsfell Hall built nearby as a farmhouse.

Helsfell Hall Two is now on the other side of the Kendal bypass, as fine a seventeenth-century house as anywhere in the Lakes. In the nineteenth century a more modern arrangement was sought when Helsfell Hall Three was built on the Windermere Road, and confusion has reigned ever since. The author can see no future for the remains of Helsfell Hall One as Kendal suburbs push out in the direction of Windermere – there is no listing or scheduling; while Helsfell Hall Two is listed its earlier original lies unprotected. Maybe this book will better inform the peripatetic professionals who really seem to have got their records in a twist at present. Helsfell Hall Three has virtually ceased to exist, as it is surrounded by a modern housing development, so only two ancient monuments now need to be considered.

This page and opposite: The panorama from the Tram footpath has changed a lot since the above picture was taken in the 1890s. The area at the end of Stricklandgate had not been developed as much, as can be seen opposite (top). The prison was still in use. It ceased to be a civil prison in 1894, but then became a military prison until it was sold to the Pennington family. The Penningtons used it as a quarry over many years, selling the ashlar blocks and worked stone to other builders in the area. Opposite, above, the main block of the prison can be seen part demolished, in about 1920. Also of interest is Dockray Hall Barn on the site of Dockray Hall, which at one time was the home of a family of equal importance to the Parr family at the castle. Unfortunately they remained Catholic at the time of Cromwell's Protectorate and lost everything. In the background can be seen the Dockray Mills with the workers' cottages nearby. The view in 2003 can be seen opposite, below.

Gillingate, at the beginning of the twentieth century, with its fine houses designed by John Flavel Curwen. These houses are visual delights, but have been difficult to maintain in the Arts and Crafts style they were built in. The field bank on the right dropped away to the Blind Beck which was not so hidden in those days. Great changes can be seen in Gillingate below as it has been developed over the years.

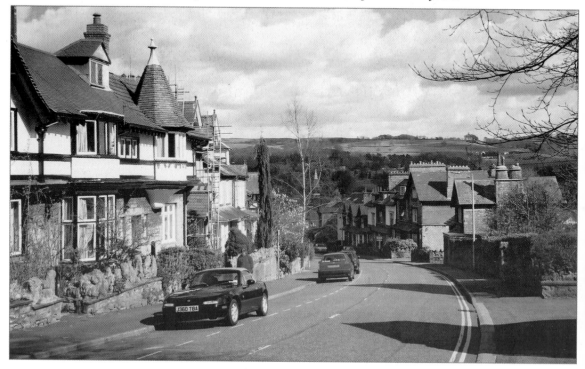

5

Finkle Street & the Old North Road

The Pump Inn and Finkle Street were so different up to the end of the nineteenth
century. It is hard to imagine that all the road traffic to the north and Scotland
squeezed down the narrow lane carrying the sign 'Finkle Street, road to station'. It
was from this narrow alley that the midnight mail coach from the north appeared
and the return coach disappeared. The Pump Inn, run by the Chorley family when
this picture was taken in the mid-nineteenth century, took its name from the town
well which was immediately at its rear in the Fish Market. The protruding building
on the right was the home of Mr Todhunter's museum and beyond was a now lost
road called Crock Lane. Finkle Street was so called as it had a slight bend in it. The
name is common in the north of England. The buildings on the right are in
Highgate and the shop on the left is in Stricklandgate. (A twenty-first-century view
can be seen on page 94.)

Finkle Street looking towards Stricklandgate in the early twentieth century, with the shop of Mr Sawyers, an early Kendal photographer who might have been more famous had he not been a socialist. He took over the fancy repository of his mother, Cecilia, added toys to the shop and took up the new art of photography, producing some first-class work much prized by collectors today, though he did not put his name on his pictures. In the background is the Liberal Club which was much expanded when the Liberal victories of 1906 called for some showing off. The modern picture is remarkable for the absence of motor vehicles.

The New Shambles was where the slaughtering of animals was moved when the Old Shambles closed in 1803. The lane was originally Watt Lane. Today the lane is much as it was a hundred years ago. The survival of such an interesting place is due entirely to half of it being owned by the Unitarian church, which refused to sell to developers who were anxious to improve the place. Today the right half of the lane looks as it did in 1803, complete with original butchers' hooks on some shops. The left side has been improved by developers and planners. The old gas light that hangs over the lane was replaced after Civic Society pressure on the council which had ideas to improve the lighting. However, it is not gas now.

The Pump Inn in 1875 when half of the buildings that blocked the top of modern Finkle Street had been removed (see page 91). The ultra-modern shelter (below) that has been erected on the site of the Pump Inn provides cover for charity workers, protesters, shoppers and bands of strolling players caught out in one of Kendal's frequent showers. The line of Crock Lane is clearly seen marked by nineteenth- and twentieth-century buildings.

Blacow's, the men's outfitters in Finkle Street, has now moved to the new shopping precinct in Elephant Yard. The business has long been a popular one and offered hosiery fitting and hat manufacture in its early days. The modern shop fronts (right) have replaced the old. The Stationery Box has gone since this picture was taken, indicating the very fluid nature of trading in modern Kendal as national companies move into the town.

Messrs R.W. and T.K. Thompson's outfitters, hatters and hosiers shop at 42–4 Finkle Street, on the corner of Branthwaite Brow, was the shop that schoolchildren attending the High School and the Grammar School had to visit for their school uniform, as no one else in town carried a stock. Messrs R.W. and T.K. were part of the Thompson family of Miles Thompson, architect from the early nineteenth century. Today schoolchildren still flock to the premises now run by O'Loughlins as a toy and model shop. Their purchases are a lot more exciting than the Kendal Green uniforms of days gone by. It's a pity the wonderful old gas light over the door of Thompson's has been removed.

Branthwaite Brow from Market Place shows a lane that was widened in 1850 to avoid the danger of fire. In the process the buildings on the right were fitted with iron plate fronts and now are the source of much interest to architectural historians. The ancient cobbled surface that the town is so proud of today is not at all obvious in the old photograph.

The town house of the Bellingham family in Stramongate has survived many changes of use since the seventeenth century. Above it is shown as Blenkhorn's Ironmonger and Grindery, but this is only one of the many businesses that have found a home in its walls. Today it houses the premises of Henry Roberts Bookshop. The exterior of the building carries one of the false date stones erected by a Kendal builder in the late nineteenth century. Mr Airey also put one of the sixteenth-century dates on premises in Kirkland, which has caused much confusion ever since. The wall advertising for Royal Daylight White Rose and American Lamp Oil shows a manufacturer intent on attracting a wide range of custom.

New Road Horse Fair was an annual event which was held on the sloping banks of the River Kent from 1852. There was also entertainment in the form of roundabouts, slides and coconut shies. The entertainment grew over the years until it took over the space where horses were sold. In the early twentieth century the horse fair became a horse show, which became part of the Westmorland Agricultural Show at Longlands. Above is the horse fair in the late nineteenth century and below the same site today, with the New Road car park all too obvious. Infrequent attempts to transform this piece of common land into something better than a car park have been howled down by commercial interests intent on filling all available space with motor cars.

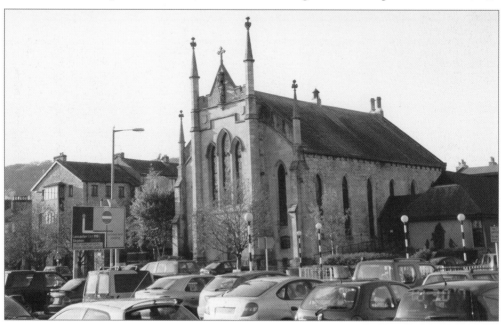

In Stramongate was the building where the Maude, Wilson and Crewdson Bank was founded on 1 January 1788 before the bank moved to the top of New Bank Yard in Highgate in 1792. The demolition of the property allowed the building of the Blackhall road (below). On the right of both pictures can be seen the Nag's Head Inn (now called the Phoenix for a reason no one, apart from the brewery owners, understands). On the left of the earlier photograph is the entrance to Blackhall Croft which, in a winding way, gave a short cut to Stricklandgate before Blackhall Road was built.

Stramongate School schoolhouse was part of a school founded by the Quakers in 1698. The school went through a number of changes until it became first a private school and then a county school. Its most famous master in Quaker days was John Dalton, the father of modern chemistry, who, it is said, worked out the atomic theory here. How the building has changed! It is now part of Grosvenor Court, which took its name from Grosvenor House – the name given to the school-house when the school closed.

St George's Church (see page 46) in its original form, with the leet that ran from the Stramongate weir to the Castle mill wheels. The bridge is where the Stock Beck joined the leet. The same scene today shows the extension added by Paley and Austin in 1907–11 to provide a new chancel and a much reduced church with no pinnacles or towers. The seat marks the site of the bridge.

This page and opposite: Stramongate yards that are no more. Yard 59 and 65 are pictured in the late nineteenth century. The modern comparisons demonstrate how today's functional architecture compares with that of times gone by. The large Provincial Insurance Co. had its headquarters in Kendal until the 1990s, and it was during its last years in the town that the two new yards were erected to accommodate their growing staff. Now Provincial has gone but the modern architecture remains.

Above: The Farmers Arms in Wildman Street was run by John Just when this picture was taken in the late nineteenth century. The pub had been the Weavers Arms and earlier the Packhorse, but it no longer exists. Sited in Doodleshire, the scene of many anti-borough council festivities, it no doubt had had its day when these festivities ceased. The Just family was listed as cowkeepers and butchers in early Kendal directories.

Below: The site today is still recognisable.

Longlands on the land between the Shap and Appleby roads was used as a summer training camp by a number of volunteer regiments that made up the army before the First World War. In the old photograph we see the Duke of Lancaster's Own Yeomanry parading for the camera of local photographer Simcoe. Except for groups of soldiers all is very rural, but times changed and the land was developed as two secondary schools with a sports track adjoining. The Kendal Horse Fair was held here before 1900. Pressure for land for commercial purposes has now produced the situation that can be seen in the new picture, where a large supermarket and other commercial buildings have been built along with car parking areas. In spite of public funding for a race track and facilities, the land remains as car parking and road.

6

Stricklandgate

Stricklandgate (or the road to Strickland Roger and Strickland Ketel) starts in Kendal town centre at the top of Finkle Street and not at the Town Hall or the Market Place. In a yard in the centre of the town called Redman's Yard (not Redmayne's as some suggest), which was next to the King's Arms Hotel, was a cottage where a group of portrait painters, which included George Romney, had a studio. In fact this is where Romney learned his trade before he left for London and international fame. The cottage which housed this amazing enterprise is shown here in the nineteenth century after it had been provided with an Arts-and-Crafts-style plaque. It is unfortunate to record that the owners of a large newspaper business on the opposite side of the yard considered the site was more valuable for the parking of three or so cars and had this most important historic building pulled down after the Second World War. The plaque was donated to Kendal Museum.

The King's Arms, Stricklandgate, was one of the famous coaching inns on the London to Scotland coaching route. Here the Royal Mail coach from the south met the Royal Mail coach from the north at midnight. There is no record of when this famous inn was built, but it is likely that it had its origins in medieval times. Its real fame came with the coaching era in the eighteenth century.

Opposite: Commercial interests destroyed the King's Arms in the 1930s when Marks & Spencer and Burton had it pulled down to make way for their shops. Even though it was a place to be proud of, no one objected to its demolition, and Kendal lost a building that many other towns would have been happy to have. This is the scene in 2003 – retail still dominates the site.

Stricklandgate from the public library in the nineteenth century and from the Market Place war memorial in the twenty-first century are, in fact, from the same place. A group of children (above) stands outside the entrance to the Wool Pack Hotel, which no longer exists, it now being the site of an American fast-food outlet. The road where John McAdam experimented with his road surfaces while he was the Turnpike Trust's engineer is empty in the nineteenth-century view, but now it suffers from daily congestion where pedestrians dodge motor transport.

The Maude Street entrance was once blocked by the house of Dr D.D. Shaw. However, in spite of its antiquity, it was demolished for the 1897 opening of Maude Street. Victorian modernisations such as this were much grander than in the twenty-first century, especially if they were connected with a jubilee of the glorious Queen Victoria, as were Maude Street and Sandes Avenue opposite.

Left: The Blackhall Brush factory of Rainforth Hodgson with its famous prickly hog sign in the nineteenth century. This original sign was given to the Museum of Lakeland Life for preservation as it was rotting. It was replaced with a replica which still stands over the traffic of today. The building is one of Kendal's amazing survivors, as all around it has perished and been replaced by modern buildings. The building dates at least to the sixteenth century when it was the townhouse of the Wilsons, one of whom became one of Kendal's first aldermen in 1565.

The Methodist church on the junction of Stricklandgate, Windermere Road and Burneside Road was built in 1808 and, until now, its appearance has been something of a mystery, as it was entirely renovated in 1883 to form the popular church building we know today. John Wesley was a frequent visitor to Kendal in the eighteenth century and a strong following built up, which still survives.

The Plumgarths Toll Booth on the Windermere road out of Kendal no longer exists, having been replaced with a large junction/terminus for the Kendal bypass which hardly merits the name of the Plumgarths Roundabout. The Turnpike Trust system of financing roads never worked as there were so many ways around most toll booths. It is not surprising that the task of road maintenance and bridge building passed to the county council in 1889. Money for roads and bridges then came from rates and taxes paid by almost everyone, whether they used the roads or not.

The Windermere Road/Burnside Road junction, in the nineteenth century, with the House of Correction Hill and Kendal Prison at the top. On the opposite side of the road was the workhouse. This mixture of fine housing and penal and Poor Law institutions did not last long into the twentieth century. First the prison closed and was demolished (see page 89) and later the workhouse became a geriatric hospital, before it too was demolished.

Below: How different the scene is now.

The building which housed Kendal Public Library was built by public subscription at the Stricklandgate end of the Market Place in 1855 as a market hall and became the library in 1891. When the modern library was erected in Stricklandgate in 1909 with money from the Carnegie charities, the old library building was demolished by the same firm that built it in 1855. The Thompson family had also moved into printing and publishing and needed a new building on land they had acquired in the new Sandes Avenue. Thus, as these three pictures illustrate, the façade and two side walls were transported to the new building in Sandes Avenue, where today it houses a shoe shop as well as the Civic Society's Kendal Local History exhibition. The exhibition was originally prepared by Mr Arthur Nicholls for the Kendal Museum and moved here after the exhibition's time expired at the Kendal Museum.

The same road junction as on page 120 but seen from Burneside Road with St Thomas's Church in the background. This church, by Websters of Kendal, was built in Fell Field and opened in 1837. As Fell Field was for many centuries a place into which the town drained, the church had to be built the wrong way round, as the tower could not be supported on the west end. This early twentieth-century view shows people standing where it would be impossible today.

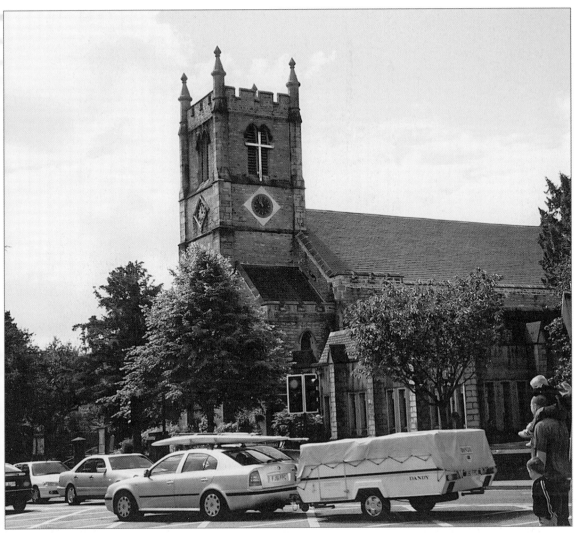

St Thomas's Church extensions of recent years can be seen here. Windermere Road-bound traffic negotiates the recently installed traffic light system.

Sandes Avenue was not built until the 1890s, and yet many of the original buildings have been replaced, sometimes more than once. The County Mews, seen here with a local coach outing in the late nineteenth-century, was replaced by the Palladium cinema by the Simpson family in the 1930s, and more recently it is the site of flats which have taken the old name 'County Mews'.

St John's Presbyterian Church was a fine building from 1897, but the site became part of the adjoining sock factory from 1981 when the United Reformed Church made it redundant. The site is now part of a complex of flats.

ACKNOWLEDGEMENTS

The production of this book would not have been possible without the assistance of the following residents of Kendal. Percy Duff has, over many years, kindly supplied me with copies of pictures from the collection of his late wife, Margaret. They were of the historic sites in the town which, like much more, have changed since the pictures were taken. As a record they are invaluable. Thanks must also go to George Dawson, who constantly made copies of interesting old pictures for my collection whenever he was able, and to Geoffrey Thompson who, on retiring from accountancy, took up modelling the lost buildings of the town, and has agreed to their exhibition in a Civic Society exhibition of the history of Kendal, which is on permanent display in the Sandes Avenue premises of Famous Footwear. Trevor Hughes has allowed me unfettered access to his late uncle's photograph collection and copied pictures from it for this book. Trevor's work for the deaf of the town is also acknowledged in this book, the proceeds of which will aid his work to provide a social club extension for the Deaf Centre building in Castle Street. Mrs Christine Strickland and her successor Mrs Jackie Fay of the Kendal County Library Local Studies Department have always given their time for whatever project I was engaged in.

PICTURE CREDITS

G. Dawson: 100, 110.

Duff Collection: 6, 17, 22, 27, 32, 34, 95, 119, 120–1, 126.

Hughes Collection: 10–11, 12 (above and below), 14, 15, 16, 18, 20, 24, 25, 26, 30, 31, 36, 37, 39, 47, 49, 50, 52, 53, 54, 56, 58, 59, 60 (above and below), 62, 63, 68, 77, 80, 81, 83, 84, 85, 88, 89, 91, 104–5, 106, 108–9, 111, 115, 116–17, 118.

Kendal Library: 21, 38, 79, 94, 97, 122.

J. Lovelace: 86.

J. Marsh: 9, 28–9, 35, 40, 41, 42, 43, 44, 45, 46, 48, 51, 57, 61, 64, 66, 67, 69, 70-1, 72, 73, 74–5, 78, 82, 86–7, 90, 92, 93, 96, 98–9, 101, 102–3, 107, 112–13, 114, 123, 124, 127.

All modern pictures were taken by the author.